MEGAN ZOSKI

Launch Without Limits

A Step-by-Step Guide to Starting and Growing a Business on a Tight Budget

This book was professionally typeset on Reedsy. Find out more at reedsy.com

Contents

Introduction

Starting a business can feel challenging, especially when you're working with limited funds. You might be asking yourself, "How can I compete with companies that have huge budgets?" or "What if I can't afford the tools and resources I need to succeed?" The good news is that starting and growing a successful business doesn't have to cost a fortune. In fact, with the right strategies, mindset, and a little creativity, you can turn your entrepreneurial dreams into reality without breaking the bank. This book is here to show you how!

Welcome to *Launch Without Limits*, your step-by-step guide to building a thriving business on a tight budget. Whether you're launching a side hustle, starting your first company, or looking for ways to grow your existing business while keeping costs low, this book is packed with practical advice and actionable strategies to help you succeed. Let's dive into what you can expect.

Funding Your Business on a Budget

One of the biggest misconceptions about starting a business is that you need a pile of cash to get started. While having access to funding can certainly make things easier, it's not a dealbreaker if you're strapped for cash. In this book, you'll learn creative ways to fund your business without taking on massive debt or seeking out investors who might expect a piece of your company in return.

From bootstrapping and personal savings to tapping into grants, crowdfunding platforms, and community resources, you'll discover how to access the money you need while staying in control of your vision. We'll also explore strategies for stretching every dollar, so you can maximize your resources and keep your business financially healthy right from the start.

Leveraging Free and Low-Cost Resources

Gone are the days when starting a business required expensive tools, offices, and staff. Thanks to the internet and the growing abundance of free and low-cost resources, it's never been easier to start small and grow strategically. Throughout this book, I'll introduce you to powerful tools and platforms that can help you market your business, manage operations, and reach customers—all without blowing your budget.

From free marketing tools like social media and email platforms to affordable website builders, productivity apps, and even free training programs, you'll learn how to build a professional business presence without paying a premium. The key is knowing where to look and how to take advantage of what's available, and that's exactly what this book will teach you.

Running Operations on a Budget

Starting a business is one thing; keeping it running smoothly is another. This is where the concept of running operations on a shoestring budget comes into play. Whether it's negotiating better deals with suppliers, outsourcing tasks to freelancers, or using automation to save time and money, you'll learn how to operate efficiently without compromising on quality or customer satisfaction.

We'll also explore how to scale your business smartly, reinvesting profits to grow sustainably while avoiding unnecessary risks. The goal isn't just to survive on a tight budget but to thrive and set your business up for long-term success.

Why This Book Matters

You're here because you have a vision—a product, service, or idea you're passionate about sharing with the world. But passion alone isn't enough; you need the tools, strategies, and confidence to make it happen. That's where this book comes in.

Launch Without Limits is more than just a guide; it's a roadmap to help you navigate the challenges of starting and growing a business with limited funds. It's about proving that big dreams don't require big budgets—just determination, resourcefulness, and a willingness to take action.

You don't need to have all the answers right now. You just need to take the first step. So let's roll up our sleeves, get creative, and show the world what's possible when you launch without limits!

Laying the Foundation: Mindset & Vision for Success

Starting a business is as much about your mindset as it is about your actions. The way you think about challenges, opportunities, and even failures will play a huge role in determining your success. In this chapter, we'll explore how to develop a growth mindset that empowers you to overcome obstacles, adapt to change, and build a resilient foundation for your business.

Shifting Your Mindset to Entrepreneurial Thinking

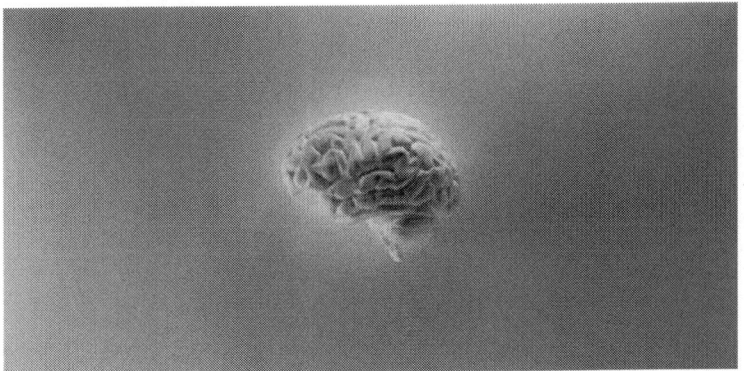

Identify Limiting Beliefs About Money and Entrepreneurship

Many of us grow up with limiting beliefs about money and what it takes to be an entrepreneur. You might think, "I need a lot of money to start a business," or "I'm not cut out to be an entrepreneur." These beliefs can hold you back before you even get started. The first step to overcoming them is identifying them.

Take a moment to reflect on the stories you tell yourself about money and business. Are they based on facts, or assumptions rooted in fear and doubt? Once you've identified these beliefs, challenge them. Replace them with empowering thoughts like, "I can learn to manage money effectively," or "Successful entrepreneurs come from all walks of life, and I'm no exception."

Reframe Challenges as Opportunities

Running a business will inevitably come with challenges, but the way you approach them can make all the difference. Instead of seeing obstacles as roadblocks, try reframing them as opportunities to learn and grow.

For example, if you're struggling to attract customers, view it as an opportunity to refine your marketing strategy and better understand your target audience. Each challenge you face is a chance to build new skills, strengthen your business, and gain confidence in your abilities. Adopting this mindset will help you stay motivated and focused, even when the going gets tough.

Cultivate Resilience Through Setbacks

Every entrepreneur experiences setbacks. Whether it's a failed product launch, a missed goal, or a financial hiccup, these moments can feel discouraging. But setbacks don't have to define your journey. Resilience is the key to bouncing back stronger.

To cultivate resilience, focus on what you can control and learn from every experience. Ask yourself, "What went wrong, and what can I do differently next time?" Surround yourself with supportive people who encourage you to keep going. And remember, every successful entrepreneur has faced setbacks— it's how you respond to them that sets you apart.

By developing a growth mindset, identifying and challenging limiting beliefs, reframing challenges, and building resilience, you'll lay a strong foundation for your business success. These mental shifts will not only help you navigate the ups and downs of entrepreneurship but also empower you to turn your vision into reality.

Embrace Resourcefulness Over Resources

Understand the Power of Leveraging Existing Skills

You don't need to be an expert in everything to start a business. Often, the skills you already have can be your biggest advantage. Take stock of your talents, experiences, and knowledge. Whether you're great at writing, designing, organizing, or connecting with people, these skills can be the foundation of your business.

For example, if you have a knack for social media, you could offer social media management services. If you're skilled at graphic design, consider creating logos or marketing materials for other businesses. The key is to identify what you're good at and find ways to monetize those skills.

Focus on Creating Value for Customers

At the heart of every successful business is the ability to solve a problem or meet a need. Instead of fixating on what you lack, focus on what you can offer. Ask yourself: What value can I provide to my customers? How can I make their lives easier, better, or more enjoyable?

By prioritizing value creation, you'll build a loyal customer base that appreciates what you bring to the table. Remember, customers care more about the benefits they receive than the resources you have. Even with limited funds, you can create exceptional value through excellent service, quality products, and personalized experiences.

Look for Creative Problem-Solving Opportunities

Entrepreneurship is essentially about solving problems. When you're working with a tight budget, you'll need to think outside the box to overcome obstacles. This might mean finding free or low-cost alternatives to expensive tools, bartering services with other entrepreneurs, or using unconventional methods to reach your goals.

For instance, if you can't afford a professional website, start with a free or low-cost platform. If marketing costs are high, leverage social media and word-of-mouth to spread the word about your business. Each challenge is an opportunity to innovate and find a solution that works within your means.

By embracing resourcefulness, you'll not only save money but also develop a mindset that drives creativity and innovation. Resourcefulness is a skill that will serve you well throughout your entrepreneurial journey, helping you adapt to challenges and seize opportunities as they arise.

Build Confidence in Starting Small

"One small step for man, one giant leap for mankind." - Neil Armstrong

Learn from Successful Entrepreneurs Who Started with Little

Take a look at some of the biggest success stories out there: Apple, Amazon, and Starbucks. These companies didn't launch with millions of dollars in funding. Steve Jobs and Steve Wozniak started Apple in a garage. Jeff Bezos ran Amazon out of his garage while packing books for orders himself. Howard Schultz grew Starbucks into a global coffee empire, beginning with a small, single location in Seattle. They all shared one thing in common: they had the confidence to start small and scale up over time. They didn't wait for everything to be perfect—they took that first step, knowing that every tiny action could eventually lead to something big.

What does this mean for you? It means that if they can do it, so can you. You don't need to wait for the "perfect" time or perfect funding to get started. Begin with what you have, learn as you go, and most importantly—don't be afraid to take that first step, no matter how small.

Redefine Success: Small Wins Lead to Big Outcomes

We often think of success as something grand: a big launch, a massive influx of customers, or an explosion of profits. While those things are definitely exciting, they don't usually happen overnight. The real secret to success is in the small wins—those everyday steps that build the foundation for bigger accomplishments down the road.

As you begin your journey, it's essential to redefine success.

11

Instead of focusing solely on grand, sweeping achievements, celebrate the smaller milestones along the way. Maybe it's securing your first customer, getting a piece of positive feedback, or finally launching your website. These small wins are proof that you're making progress, and each one brings you closer to your bigger goals.

Establish a Sustainable Long-Term Mindset

When you're operating with a tight budget, it's easy to get caught up in short-term thinking: How can I make quick sales? How can I turn a profit fast? But the key to success isn't just about quick wins—it's about building a sustainable business that will thrive over time.

Instead of obsessing over short-term gains, focus on creating a business model that can grow and evolve. Think about how you can offer value to your customers consistently. Focus on creating strong customer relationships, improving your product or service bit by bit, and keeping an eye on long-term goals. A business that is built with a sustainable mindset is one that will last and flourish, even when the going gets tough.

The truth is, growing a business on a budget is a marathon, not a sprint. It's about laying a solid foundation and making thoughtful, intentional decisions that will pay off over time. Embrace this mindset, and you'll find yourself more confident and prepared for the journey ahead. Starting small doesn't mean staying small—it's the first step toward building something big and lasting.

Crafting a Lean Business Plan That Works

When you're starting a business on a tight budget, you may feel like you need a thick, complicated business plan to get started. But the truth is, less is often more. That's where a lean business plan comes in—a streamlined, efficient approach that focuses on the essentials without the fluff. It's the perfect solution for entrepreneurs who need a clear direction but don't have the time or resources to dive into a more elaborate plan.

Understanding the Basics of a Lean Business Plan

Overview of the One-Page Business Plan Model

A lean business plan isn't about writing pages and pages of strategy and market analysis. Instead, it's about clarity, simplicity, and focus. One of the most popular models is the one-page business plan. As the name suggests, it distills everything you need to know into a single page. This makes it easy to reference, update, and share with potential partners, investors, or mentors.

The beauty of the one-page business plan is that it allows you to focus on what's truly important: the core elements that will drive your business forward. No fluff, just the essentials that can guide you on your path from idea to profitable business.

Key Components of a Simple Yet Effective Plan

Even though it's short, a one-page business plan should still cover the essential components that will guide your business. Here's what to include:

1. **Mission Statement**: What is the purpose of your business? Why does it exist? A clear mission statement will help keep your focus sharp as you build your brand.
2. **Value Proposition**: What makes your business different from others? What problem are you solving for your customers? Your value proposition should highlight what sets you apart and why customers should choose you. *See subsection A for further information.
3. **Target Market**: Who are your ideal customers? Be

specific about who you're serving, their needs, and why they're a good fit for your product or service. *See subsection B for further information.

4. **Revenue Model**: How will you make money? Whether it's through product sales, subscription services, or something else, this section should clarify how your business will generate income. *See subsection C for further information.

5. **Marketing and Sales Strategy**: How will you attract and retain customers? Keep your marketing plan simple but focused on the methods that will work best for your target audience.

6. **Key Milestones and Goals**: What are your short-term and long-term goals? Break them down into actionable steps that will guide your progress over time.

7. **Financial Overview**: A basic financial forecast will help you understand your cash flow, expenses, and profitability. You don't need to create a detailed financial statement, but a rough estimate of your income and expenses will provide useful insight.

Outline Your Unique Value Proposition Succinctly

Your unique value proposition (UVP) is what sets your business apart from the competition. It's the reason why customers should choose you over others—and it's essential to define it clearly and concisely. A strong UVP will communicate the benefits of your product or service in a way that resonates with your target market and makes you stand out in a crowded marketplace.

To craft your UVP, ask yourself:

- **What problem does my business solve?** Focus on the pain points that your product or service addresses for your customers.
- **How do I solve it differently or better than anyone else?** This is where you highlight your differentiators—what makes your product or service unique.
- **What is the benefit to the customer?** Focus on the outcome or transformation your customer will experience by using your product or service.

Keep your UVP short, simple, and direct. Avoid jargon or long-winded explanations. Think of it as your "elevator pitch"—the sentence or two you could share with someone in a short amount of time that leaves them wanting to learn more.

A good example could be: "We provide eco-friendly, affordable skincare products that help people feel confident and care for their skin without harming the environment." This clearly states what they offer, who they're helping, and how they're different from other skincare brands.

Define Your Target Market Clearly

Knowing exactly who you're serving is the first step in building a business that resonates with customers. Without a clear target market, it's like trying to hit a moving target blindfolded—you might get lucky, but it's much harder to achieve consistent success.

To define your target market clearly, think about the following:

17

- **Demographics**: What age, gender, income level, and education do your ideal customers typically have? This will give you a clear picture of who you're reaching.
- **Psychographics**: What are their values, interests, and lifestyles? What problems or needs do they have that your business can solve? Understanding your customer's mindset helps you connect with them on a deeper level.
- **Geographics**: Where are your customers located? Are you serving a local, regional, national, or global audience? This will influence your marketing and distribution strategies.

The more specific you can get with your target market, the more effective your marketing will be. Instead of trying to reach "everyone," focus on a smaller, well-defined group of people who are most likely to benefit from your product or service. The clearer you are on who your audience is, the easier it will be to create products, messaging, and offers that directly meet their needs.

Identify the Initial Products or Services to Offer

One of the toughest decisions when starting a business is deciding what to offer first. It can be tempting to offer a wide range of products or services, but remember: the goal at the beginning is to keep things manageable while you get your feet wet and learn the ropes. Start by identifying a small, targeted selection of products or services that align with your UVP and the needs of your target market.

Consider the following when choosing what to offer initially (the next section focuses on this):

- **Solve a specific problem**: Make sure your products or services are designed to solve a clear problem for your target audience. The more focused you can be, the easier it will be to market and sell.
- **Test the waters**: It's okay to start small with a limited product offering. This gives you the chance to test customer reactions, get feedback, and make improvements before you expand.
- **Be realistic about resources**: When working with a tight budget, it's important to choose products or services that are realistic to produce, distribute, and maintain. Focus on what you can handle with the resources you have available.
- **Focus on quality over quantity**: It's better to offer a few high-quality products or services than to overwhelm yourself with too many options. This will help you build a strong reputation with your customers from the start.

Once you've identified your initial offerings, keep your product or service offerings aligned with your UVP and mission. They should make sense for your target market and provide clear value. As you grow, you can always expand your offerings, but getting the foundation right will set you up for long-term success.

Benefits of Keeping Plans Adaptable and Flexible

One of the biggest benefits of a lean business plan is that it's adaptable. As you start your business, you'll inevitably encounter new challenges, opportunities, and shifts in the market. Having a lean plan allows you to pivot as needed without being bogged down by an overly detailed, rigid strategy.

In fact, flexibility is key when running a business on a tight budget. You might discover that your initial assumptions about your target audience, pricing, or marketing tactics need to be adjusted. The lean business plan allows you to make those changes quickly and easily without losing sight of your overall goals.

Being adaptable also means you can respond to customer feedback more effectively. If customers are asking for features or services you hadn't planned for, your lean plan allows you to make adjustments without starting from scratch. This kind of flexibility will help you stay agile and resilient as your business grows.

Step-By-Step: Setting Up Your Business Strategy in 9 Steps

Step 1: Understand Your Customer's Pain Points

Before you can offer a solution, you first need to understand the problem. What are the specific pain points or challenges your target audience is facing? These are the frustrations, roadblocks, or unmet needs that drive people to seek out products or services like yours.

To get a clear picture of their pain points, start by:

- **Listening to your audience**: Pay attention to what your potential customers are saying in conversations, online forums, social media, or customer reviews of similar products or services. What are they struggling with? What do they wish existed to make their lives easier?

- **Conducting informal research**: You don't need a huge budget to conduct customer research. Start by having informal conversations with your friends, family, or acquaintances who fit your target market. Ask them about their biggest challenges and frustrations related to your business idea.

- **Empathizing with your customers**: Put yourself in their shoes. What does a typical day look like for them? What is the emotional impact of the pain they're experiencing? The more you can empathize with their situation, the more effectively you can craft a solution that truly resonates.

Understanding your customers' pain points is the foundation of your business. It's what informs every decision you make, from product development to marketing strategy. If you can pinpoint the problem clearly, you'll be in a better position to offer a compelling solution.

Step 2: Build Solutions Tailored to Their Needs

Once you understand your customers' pain points, it's time to build a solution that meets their needs. A successful business is one that not only solves a problem but does so in a way that is convenient, valuable, and effective for your customers.

Here's how to tailor your solutions:

- **Keep it simple and focused**: Start with a product or service that addresses the most pressing need of your target audience. Avoid overcomplicating things—when you're working with a tight budget, simplicity is key. Offer a streamlined solution that does one thing really well.
- **Solve their problem effectively**: Your offering should directly solve the pain points you identified. Focus on making your product or service the best possible solution for your customers' needs, even if it's a small, niche offering.
- **Communicate the benefit**: When marketing your solution, always focus on the benefit, not just the features. Show your customers how your product or service will make their lives easier, save them time, reduce their stress, or solve their specific problem in a meaningful way.

Building a solution that directly addresses customer needs is one of the most effective ways to build trust, loyalty, and long-term relationships. By staying laser-focused on what your customers truly want, you'll be more likely to create an offering that resonates and sells.

Step 3: Use Surveys and Early Feedback to Shape Your Offering

One of the best ways to make sure you're on the right track is by getting direct feedback from your customers early on. Whether you're just starting out or have launched a product or service, gathering feedback from real customers helps you understand what's working, what's not, and what you can improve.

Here are some ways to gather valuable insights:

- **Send out surveys**: Use simple online tools like Google Forms or SurveyMonkey to create quick surveys that ask customers what they think about your product or service. Ask questions like, "What was most helpful about our offering?" or "What improvements would make it better for you?" Surveys can give you specific, actionable data to improve your product.

- **Conduct one-on-one interviews**: If possible, have direct conversations with your early customers. Ask open-ended questions to dive deeper into their experience. You'll gain a more nuanced understanding of their thoughts and feelings about your business.

- **Monitor customer behavior**: Pay attention to how your customers interact with your website, social media, or product. Are they asking questions? What parts are they engaging with the most? This kind of data can give you clues about what's resonating and what needs improvement.

- **Improve based on feedback**: Take what you learn and use it to refine your product or service. Early feedback is a powerful tool for improvement—don't be afraid to make adjustments based on what your customers are telling you. The more adaptable you are, the more likely you are to succeed in the long run.

Gathering feedback from your customers not only helps you improve your offerings but also shows your customers that you care about their needs. When customers feel heard and valued, they're more likely to become loyal advocates for your business.

Creating a customer-focused strategy isn't about guessing what your customers want; it's about actively listening, understanding their pain points, and building solutions that make a real difference. By continually gathering feedback and adapting your offerings, you can stay connected to your customers and ensure that you're always meeting their evolving needs. A customer-centric approach will not only help you grow your business on a tight budget but also build lasting relationships that fuel your success.

Step 4: Use Competitive Analysis to Set Reasonable Pricing

When you're just starting, pricing can feel like a guessing game. But don't worry—you don't have to figure it out on your own. One of the best ways to set reasonable pricing is to look at your competitors. Competitive analysis helps you understand where your product or service fits in the market and what customers are willing to pay.

Here's how to use competitive analysis to set your pricing:

- **Identify key competitors**: Research businesses that offer similar products or services in your niche. Pay attention to their pricing structures, especially those that seem most similar to your own offerings.
- **Understand their pricing strategy**: Are they using premium pricing because they offer high-end features? Or do they offer a more affordable solution aimed at budget-conscious customers? Understanding their approach can give you a sense of where your pricing should fall.
- **Evaluate the value you provide**: Consider how your

offering compares to competitors in terms of quality, features, and benefits. If you offer something unique or different, you might be able to price higher. If you're offering a more basic solution, pricing lower could help attract price-sensitive customers.

- **Factor in your costs**: Remember to also consider your production, marketing, and operational costs when setting your price. The goal is to cover your expenses while ensuring you're pricing competitively and fairly.

Competitive analysis helps you set a reasonable starting point for your prices, but keep in mind that pricing isn't set in stone. You can always adjust as you learn more about your customers' willingness to pay and what the market demands.

Step 5: Test Pricing Models for Profitability

When working with a tight budget, profitability is key. But how do you know if your pricing model is working? The answer lies in testing. Pricing isn't a one-size-fits-all strategy, and it's okay to experiment with different models until you find the one that maximizes your profit and appeals to your customers.

Here are a few ways to test your pricing model:

- **Offer tiered pricing**: A tiered pricing model offers different levels of pricing based on the features, services, or products included. This allows you to test different price points and see which resonates most with your audience. For example, you could offer a basic version at a lower price and a premium version with added features at a higher price.

- **Use promotional pricing**: Consider offering a limited-time promotion or discount to test the response of your target market. This can help you gauge demand and understand if a higher price would be acceptable after the promotion ends.
- **A/B testing**: Try offering the same product at different price points to see which one attracts more customers. Keep all other factors constant and test small variations over a set period of time to gather data on pricing effectiveness.
- **Track customer feedback**: After testing different pricing models, gather feedback from customers to understand if they find the pricing fair and what additional value they would expect for a higher price.

Don't be afraid to adjust as you go. Testing allows you to find the pricing model that maximizes profitability while also staying aligned with your customers' expectations and needs.

Step 6: Define Initial Revenue Benchmarks

Once you've settled on your pricing strategy, it's time to define your revenue goals. Setting clear revenue benchmarks helps you track your progress, measure success, and stay motivated as you work to grow your business. Without specific revenue targets, it can be hard to know if you're on the right path.

Here's how to define your initial revenue benchmarks:

- **Start with realistic goals**: Your first revenue targets should be achievable, given your market, product, and resources. Start small and aim for steady growth rather than setting lofty goals that might be out of reach.

- **Consider your pricing and sales targets**: Use your pricing model to calculate how many sales you need to hit your revenue goals. For example, if you're selling a product for $50 and your goal is $5,000 in revenue, you'll need to sell 100 units.

- **Set short-term and long-term goals**: While it's important to have a clear target for the first few months, think about your long-term revenue goals as well. For the first 3-6 months, your focus might be on building a customer base and breaking even, but long-term goals should reflect growth and profitability as you scale.

- **Track key metrics**: Break your revenue goals down into smaller, manageable metrics, such as monthly sales, customer acquisition rates, and average order value. Tracking these metrics will give you insight into your progress and allow you to adjust your strategy as needed.

- **Monitor cash flow**: Revenue goals are important, but so is maintaining healthy cash flow. Ensure that you're covering your costs and leaving room for reinvestment in your business. Having a solid cash flow plan will help you avoid running into financial trouble as you grow.

Defining your revenue benchmarks early on will keep you focused and allow you to measure your progress toward your bigger goals. As your business grows, you'll continue to refine your benchmarks to reflect new levels of success.

Step 7: Set Realistic Short-Term Goals for 6-12 Months

In the early stages of your business, your focus should be on building a solid foundation. Setting clear, realistic short-term goals will give you a sense of direction and provide measurable milestones that indicate whether you're on track.

Here's how to set those goals:

- **Define key objectives**: Think about what you want to achieve in the first 6-12 months. This could be anything from reaching a certain number of customers, launching a website, or achieving a specific revenue target. Whatever your goals, make sure they are measurable so you can track progress.
- **Be realistic and specific**: Avoid overloading yourself with too many goals. Focus on a few that you can realistically achieve in your given time frame. For example, if your business is still in the product development phase, set goals around completing prototypes, testing, or securing your first paying customers.
- **Break goals down into actionable steps**: Once you've defined your goals, break them down into smaller, actionable steps. For instance, if your goal is to reach a specific revenue target, you'll need to identify how many sales you need to make each month to hit that number. These smaller steps help you stay focused and make progress each day.
- **Track progress regularly**: Set a schedule to review your progress at least monthly. This allows you to identify any obstacles early on and make adjustments as needed. Regular tracking ensures you stay on course and motivated to reach

your milestones.

Setting these short-term goals gives you a clear path to follow in the first year and ensures you're building momentum without trying to take on too much too soon.

Step 8: Plan Strategies for Scaling Operations Later

Once you've established a solid foundation in the early months, it's time to start thinking about how you'll scale your business. Scaling is about growing your operations efficiently without compromising quality or customer satisfaction. Planning for growth in advance helps you avoid overwhelming yourself and gives you a roadmap for handling increased demand.

Consider the following strategies for scaling later:

- **Assess operational needs**: Look at your current operations and identify areas where you'll need to expand in order to meet growing demand. This could include hiring staff, investing in new technology, or increasing your inventory. Be sure to understand the areas that will need to be upgraded before scaling your business.
- **Automate and streamline**: As your business grows, repetitive tasks can start to take up a lot of your time. Look for ways to automate processes like email marketing, accounting, customer support, and inventory management. This will help you focus more on strategic decisions while keeping operations running smoothly.
- **Develop strategic partnerships**: One way to scale without taking on too much risk is to form partnerships with

other businesses or influencers. Strategic partnerships can help you access new markets, increase sales, or add new value to your products or services without having to do it all yourself.

- **Build a scalable marketing plan**: As your business grows, so should your marketing efforts. Develop strategies that are scalable, such as social media ads, email campaigns, or content marketing. These efforts can be expanded over time as you have more resources to invest in them.

Scaling is about preparing your business to handle more customers and higher demand while ensuring that you can continue delivering great products and services. By planning ahead, you'll have a better understanding of when and how to expand your operations effectively.

Step 9: Balance Growth with Manageable Workloads

It's easy to get caught up in the excitement of growth, but rapid expansion can quickly lead to burnout and inefficiencies if you're not careful. When you're on a tight budget, it's especially important to balance your growth with a workload that's manageable, ensuring you don't overextend yourself too soon.

Here are a few ways to balance growth with manageable workloads:

- **Set realistic growth expectations**: Don't feel pressured to scale faster than you can handle. It's important to pace yourself and grow at a rate that matches your resources, capabilities, and team size. Stretching yourself too thin can lead to mistakes, poor customer service, or burnout.

- **Delegate and outsource**: As your business grows, you may need to delegate tasks to free up your time for higher-priority activities. This doesn't always mean hiring full-time employees; you can outsource tasks like graphic design, copywriting, or bookkeeping to freelancers. This keeps your workload manageable while allowing you to focus on strategy and growth.

- **Focus on profitability, not just revenue**: While growing your revenue is important, focus on building a profitable business that doesn't drain your resources. Make sure you're not sacrificing profitability for the sake of rapid growth. It's better to grow slowly and sustainably than to expand too quickly and risk financial instability.

- **Know when to take a step back**: Sometimes the best thing you can do for your business is to slow down. If you're feeling overwhelmed, take a moment to reassess your goals and resources. Taking the time to pause and evaluate will help you make more informed decisions and prevent burnout.

Mapping out a growth timeline is a strategic process that combines short-term goals, long-term scalability, and careful balance. By setting realistic expectations for the first 6-12 months, planning for future scaling, and balancing growth with a manageable workload, you'll ensure that your business can grow at a steady pace without losing focus or overextending yourself. With the right plan in place, you'll be ready to build the foundation for lasting success.

Preparing For Launch

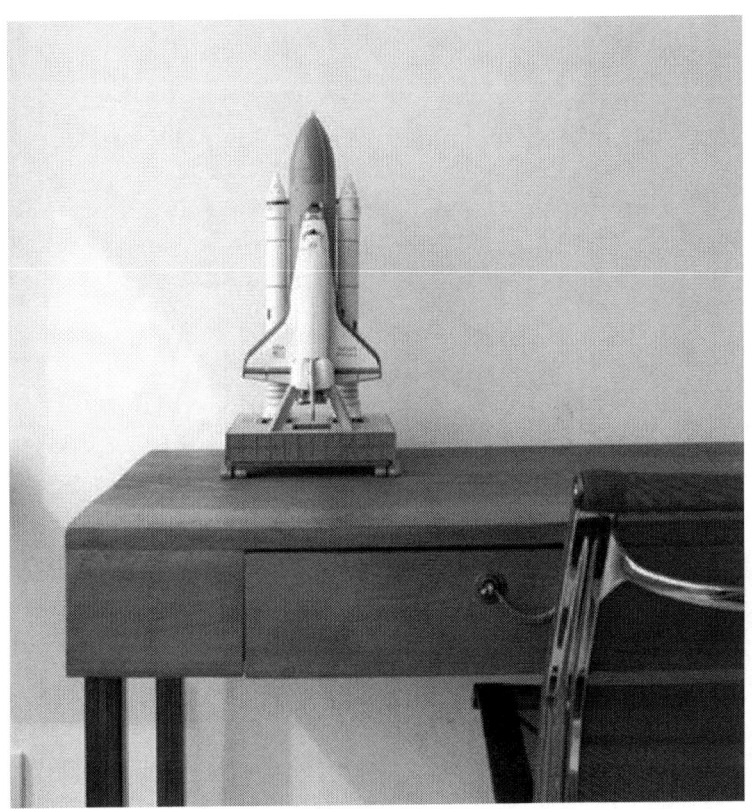

Validate Your Business Concept One Last Time

Before diving into full-scale operations, it's crucial to validate your business concept one last time. This is the moment when you get to test whether your product or service truly meets the market's needs.

Let's explore how to conduct this final validation to ensure you're on the right track before committing all your time and resources.

Test the Market Demand with a Pre-Launch Campaign

A pre-launch campaign is a powerful way to test the waters and gauge market demand before fully committing to your business. It allows you to gather early feedback, generate excitement, and see if there's real interest in your offering.

Here's how to run an effective pre-launch campaign:

- **Create buzz and excitement**: Use social media, email marketing, and your website to tease your product or service. Share sneak peeks, behind-the-scenes footage, or countdowns leading up to the launch. This builds anticipation and gets potential customers excited about what you have to offer.
- **Offer early access or discounts**: Give a select group of people early access to your product, or offer a limited-time discount in exchange for their feedback or commitment to buy. This not only helps you generate sales but also builds trust and loyalty among your early supporters.
- **Collect contact information**: Make it easy for interested prospects to sign up for updates or early access. This allows you to create a list of potential customers you can target when you officially launch. The more interest you gather, the more you'll know about demand before your official

rollout.

- **Engage with your audience**: Encourage your followers to ask questions, share thoughts, and provide feedback on your pre-launch content. Responding to comments and interacting with potential customers helps build relationships and creates a sense of community around your brand.

By testing the market demand with a pre-launch campaign, you're getting valuable insights about whether your offering is truly needed and how much excitement exists in your target market.

Address Any Red Flags from Feedback Received

No business idea is perfect, and it's inevitable that you'll receive some negative or constructive feedback along the way. However, rather than being discouraged, use this feedback to address any potential red flags and refine your offering.

Here's how to respond to feedback effectively:

- **Listen carefully**: When people point out issues or concerns, listen with an open mind. Whether it's a problem with your product, service, pricing, or messaging, it's essential to understand where your concept might fall short and why it's raising doubts.
- **Look for recurring patterns**: If multiple people are pointing out the same issue, this is a clear sign that it needs to be addressed. Is there a specific feature missing? Is the value proposition unclear? Or are there concerns about the

price? Pay attention to trends in the feedback.

- **Make adjustments**: Use the feedback to fine-tune your offering. If you discover a major red flag, such as customers not fully understanding the value of your product, it might be time to rethink your messaging. If you receive concerns about a feature, you may need to reconsider your product design or functionality.
- **Communicate changes**: Once you've addressed any issues, be transparent with your audience. Let them know that you've listened to their feedback and made changes based on it. This shows that you value their opinions and are committed to delivering a better product.

Addressing red flags early in the process helps ensure that you're on the right track and can prevent potential problems from becoming bigger issues down the line.

Confirm Product-Market Fit Before Full Commitment

One of the most critical steps in validating your business concept is confirming that there is a true product-market fit.

Consider the following:

- **Measure interest and demand**: Look at how many people are signing up for your pre-launch campaign or showing interest in your offering. Are people willing to commit to purchasing your product? If you're getting strong engagement and conversions, that's a sign that your product is appealing to your target market.

- **Check for willingness to pay**: One of the most powerful indicators of product-market fit is whether people are willing to pay for your product. If you're offering early access or a discount, gauge how many people actually follow through and purchase. If they're hesitant or reluctant to buy, it may indicate that there's a disconnect between the product and the market need.
- **Review customer feedback**: Beyond just interest, product-market fit is confirmed when customers genuinely love your product, keep using it, and recommend it to others. If you receive positive, enthusiastic feedback from your early users and they're willing to share their experiences, that's a strong sign of product-market fit.
- **Adjust based on the feedback**: Sometimes, confirming product-market fit may require some iteration. If you find that there's strong interest but some feedback suggests improvements, don't be afraid to tweak your product or service before fully committing to a larger launch.

Validating your business concept one last time before full commitment is essential for minimizing risk and ensuring that your business has the potential for success. By testing market demand with a pre-launch campaign, addressing any red flags from feedback, and confirming product-market fit, you're setting yourself up for a smoother and more confident launch. These final validation steps give you the clarity and confidence to move forward with your business and make a lasting impact in your market.

Create an Actionable Launch Checklist

Once you've validated your business concept and are ready to take the leap, it's time to create a detailed and actionable checklist to ensure that your launch runs smoothly. This checklist will keep you organized, help you avoid missing any critical steps, and ensure that you're prepared for success from day one. The key is to tackle the essential tasks that will lay a strong foundation for your business while keeping things lean and cost-efficient.

Let's dive into the crucial steps you'll need to take to prepare for launch.

Register Your Business and Handle Legal Necessities

Before you start marketing your product or offering services, make sure your business is legally registered and in compliance with the necessary regulations. Taking care of the legal aspects ensures that you're protected, can operate smoothly, and avoid potential pitfalls down the road.

Disclaimer: This information is for entertainment purposes only. You should not act on the basis of any content included in this section without first seeking legal or other professional advice.

Here's what to do:

- **Choose a business structure**: Decide whether you want to register as a sole proprietorship, LLC (limited liability company), corporation, or another structure. Each comes with its own set of advantages, depending on factors like liability protection, taxes, and how you plan to grow your business.

- **Register your business name**: If you haven't already, register your business name with the appropriate authorities. This establishes your business identity and protects you from anyone else using the same name.
- **Get an EIN (Employer Identification Number) or BIN (Business Identification Number)**: Apply for an EIN from the IRS if you're in the United States or a Business Identification Number if you're in Canada. This number is used for tax purposes and is necessary if you have employees or plan to hire in the future. You may also need tax numbers depending on provincial and territorial requirements.
- **Check licensing and permits**: Depending on your business type and location, you may need specific licenses or permits to operate legally. This can include health permits, sales tax permits, or zoning permits, so make sure you check with your local government.
- **Consult with a lawyer or accountant**: If you're unsure about any legal or tax implications, it's worth consulting with a professional to ensure you're set up correctly from the start.

Taking care of the legal necessities upfront will give you peace of mind and allow you to focus on growing your business once you launch.

Set Up Lean Operations for Cost-Efficiency

With limited funds, keeping your operations lean is essential for maintaining a healthy cash flow and focusing your resources on what matters most: serving your customers. Set up cost-efficient systems that will enable you to operate smoothly while minimizing expenses.

Here's how to set up lean operations:

- **Simplify your processes**: Identify the core processes that are essential to running your business and streamline them. This could involve automating repetitive tasks, using software tools to manage inventory or customer data, or finding ways to cut out unnecessary steps in your workflow.
- **Outsource non-core tasks**: Instead of hiring full-time staff for every function, consider outsourcing tasks like accounting, marketing, or customer support to freelancers or contractors. This saves you the overhead of full-time employees while still allowing you to get the work done.
- **Invest in affordable tools**: Use affordable software and tools that can help you manage your business efficiently. Look for all-in-one solutions that cover your needs, such as project management, invoicing, customer relationship management (CRM), and marketing. There are plenty of low-cost or even free tools that can help you run operations smoothly.
- **Minimize inventory costs**: If you're selling physical products, start with minimal inventory and scale as demand increases. You can also look into drop shipping or print-on-demand services to reduce the upfront investment and

storage costs.

By keeping operations lean, you'll free up resources to reinvest in other important areas of your business, such as marketing, customer acquisition, or product development.

Build a Strong Online and Local Presence

In today's world, building a strong online presence is critical, but don't overlook the value of local visibility, especially if you're targeting a community or region. Combining both will give you a comprehensive strategy for attracting customers and growing your brand.

Here's how to build your online and local presence:

- **Launch a professional website**: Your website is the face of your business. Ensure it's user-friendly, mobile-optimized, and clearly communicates your value proposition. Include essential information like your services or products, contact details, and any promotions. You can use website builders like Wix, WordPress, or Squarespace to create a professional-looking website without a hefty price tag.
- **Set up social media profiles**: Create social media profiles on platforms like Instagram, Facebook, LinkedIn, or TikTok, depending on where your target audience spends their time. Post regularly and engage with your followers by responding to comments, sharing relevant content, and building relationships.

- **Leverage local SEO**: To build a local presence, make sure your business is visible in local search results. Set up and optimize your Google My Business profile, ensuring that your address, hours, and contact information are accurate. Encourage local reviews and ratings from your customers, as this will help you appear in local searches.
- **Attend local events or networking groups**: If you're targeting a local community, attend networking events, local trade shows, or workshops where you can meet potential customers and partners. You can also consider hosting your own event or meet-up to build awareness in your area.
- **Utilize online ads**: Paid advertising, such as Google Ads or Facebook Ads, can be an effective way to generate leads and attract traffic to your website. Start with a small budget, track your results, and adjust as needed.
- **Collaborate with influencers or local businesses**: Reach out to local influencers or other businesses that align with your brand to cross-promote. A partnership or collaboration can help you tap into their audience and increase brand awareness.

By building a strong online and local presence, you'll create a solid foundation for attracting customers and generating buzz around your brand, both in the digital space and within your community.

Bootstrap Basics: Leveraging Low-Cost Strategies

The simplest way to fund your business is to use what you already have. While it might require some sacrifice or careful planning, starting with personal savings allows you to maintain full control of your business and avoid debt.

Funding Your Business on a Budget

Explore low-cost funding options

Use Personal Savings or Reinvest Profits

How to maximize this approach:

- **Set a clear budget:** Before tapping into your savings, determine exactly how much you can afford to invest without jeopardizing your personal financial security.
- **Start small:** Use your savings to cover only the essentials— focus on what's needed to create your product and test your concept.
- **Reinvest early profits:** As your business begins to generate revenue, reinvest those profits back into the business to fund growth. For example, you can use earnings to improve your product, expand your marketing efforts, or build a larger inventory.

Seek Microloans or Crowdfunding Opportunities

Microloans:

- Microloans are small loans often provided by nonprofit organizations, community lenders, or government programs specifically designed for startups and small businesses.
- They typically come with lower interest rates and more flexible terms compared to traditional loans.
- Search online for companies that offer them or contact your local municipal office for microloan opportunities.

Crowdfunding:

- Platforms like Kickstarter, Indiegogo, or GoFundMe allow you to raise funds by appealing directly to your target audience.
- Create a compelling campaign that explains your business, shares your story, and offers rewards to backers (such as early access to your product or exclusive discounts).
- Crowdfunding not only helps you raise money but also builds an early customer base and generates buzz around your brand.

Partner with Investors Offering Sweat Equity

What is sweat equity?

Sweat equity is when someone invests their time, skills, or effort into your business instead of (or in addition to) financial capital. This approach is ideal for securing help with areas like marketing, product development, or operations without a significant cash outlay.

How to find the right partner:

- Look for individuals who share your vision and bring complementary skills to the table. For example, if you're a creative entrepreneur, consider partnering with someone who has strong financial or operational expertise.
- Clearly define roles and responsibilities upfront. Ensure there's a mutual understanding of what each partner will contribute and how equity will be divided.
- Formalize the agreement in writing. Create a partnership

or equity agreement that outlines the terms of the arrangement to avoid misunderstandings later.

Start lean to reduce startup costs

Focus on Essential Tools and Resources

- **Identify your must-haves:** Make a list of the tools, resources, and equipment that are absolutely critical for delivering your product or service. Ask yourself: "What do I need to operate today?"
- **Postpone non-essentials:** Save non-essential purchases for later, once your business generates consistent revenue. This might include upgrades, premium software, or additional tools that are "nice-to-have" but not necessary initially.
- **Start with a minimum viable product (MVP):** Instead of perfecting every aspect of your product or service, focus on launching with a basic version that solves your customers' immediate pain points. You can refine and expand over time based on feedback and revenue growth.

Rent or Borrow Equipment When Possible

- **Rent instead of buy:** Many companies offer rental services for business equipment like computers, cameras, machinery, or tools. Renting allows you to access high-quality equipment without the upfront investment.
- **Borrow from your network:** If you have friends, family, or colleagues with equipment you can use temporarily, don't hesitate to ask. Borrowing saves money and can help

you get started without committing to a purchase.

- **Buy used or refurbished:** If you must purchase equipment, look for used or refurbished options. Websites like eBay, Craigslist, or Facebook Marketplace often have affordable options in good condition.

Use Free or Inexpensive Software and Tools

- **Website creation:** Platforms like Wix, Squarespace, or WordPress offer affordable plans for building professional websites. Many include templates, hosting, and basic e-commerce functionality.
- **Marketing tools:** Use free tools like Canva for designing social media posts and flyers, Mailchimp for email marketing, and Buffer or Hootsuite for social media scheduling.
- **Project management:** Free tools like Trello or Asana can help you stay organized, track tasks, and manage your team's workload.
- **Accounting and invoicing:** FreshBooks, Wave, or Zoho Books offer affordable or free plans for tracking expenses, sending invoices, and managing your finances.
- **Communication:** Utilize free platforms like Slack, Zoom, or Google Workspace to collaborate with your team and communicate with customers.

Avoid Financial Pitfalls

Monitor Cash Flow Closely

- **Track income and expenses regularly:** Use accounting software like QuickBooks, Wave, or Xero to monitor transactions, create reports, and gain insight into your financial health.

- **Maintain a cash flow forecast:** Project your expected income and expenses for the next 3-6 months to identify potential gaps and plan accordingly.
- **Collect payments promptly:** Don't let unpaid invoices pile up. Set clear payment terms for customers and follow up on overdue payments to maintain a steady cash flow.
- **Cut unnecessary expenses:** Regularly review your spending and identify areas where you can save. For example, negotiate with vendors, switch to lower-cost tools & software, or eliminate services you're not using.

Avoid Taking on Unnecessary Debt Early On

- **Borrow only what you truly need:** Avoid the temptation to take out large loans or max out credit lines just because they're available. Focus on borrowing only enough to cover essential startup costs.
- **Explore low-interest options:** If you do need funding, look for low-interest or no-interest options such as microloans, grants, or 0% introductory-rate credit cards.
- **Prioritize reinvesting profits:** Instead of relying on borrowed funds to grow your business, use profits from early sales to fund expansion whenever possible.
- **Understand the terms:** Before taking on any debt, make sure you understand the repayment terms, interest rates, and any potential fees. This will help you avoid hidden costs that could strain your finances.

Set Aside an Emergency Fund

- **Start small and build gradually:** Aim to set aside at least 3-6 months' worth of operating expenses. If that feels overwhelming, start by saving a small percentage of your revenue each month.
- **Keep it separate:** Store your emergency fund in a separate business savings account to ensure you don't dip into it for everyday expenses.
- **Replenish after use:** If you ever need to tap into your emergency fund, prioritize replenishing it as soon as possible.

With a strong handle on your finances, you'll not only avoid potential setbacks but also create the flexibility and confidence needed to seize opportunities and build your business with success in mind.

Leveraging Free and Low-Cost Resources

Free marketing channels

Use Social Media to Build an Online Presence

- **Choose the right platforms:** Focus on the social media platforms where your target audience is most active. For example, Instagram works well for visually-driven brands, while LinkedIn is ideal for B2B businesses.
- **Create valuable content:** Share posts that resonate with your audience, such as tips, tutorials, behind-the-scenes looks, or success stories. Aim to educate, entertain, or inspire rather than just sell.
- **Engage with your audience:** Respond to comments,

answer questions, and interact with followers to build relationships and foster trust.

- **Use hashtags strategically:** Hashtags help your content reach a broader audience. Research trending and relevant hashtags for your niche to increase visibility.
- **Leverage free tools:** Use free social media tools like Canva for designing eye-catching posts and videos, or Later and Buffer to schedule your content in advance.

Network Through Community Groups or Forums

- **Local community groups:** Attend meetups, join local business associations, or participate in community events to connect with people in your area. Many communities also have Facebook or WhatsApp groups dedicated to local businesses.
- **Online forums and niche communities:** Platforms like Reddit, Quora, or industry-specific forums are great places to interact with people who might be interested in your product or service. Join discussions, answer questions, and provide value without being overly promotional.
- **Volunteer or sponsor events:** Offer your time or expertise to community events, which can raise awareness of your brand and establish your reputation as a helpful, reliable business.

Collaborate With Other Small Businesses for Exposure

- **Cross-promote on social media:** Partner with another business to share each other's content, shoutouts, or promotions with your respective audiences.

- **Bundle products or services:** Create joint offerings that combine your product or service with another business's. For example, a fitness coach could team up with a nutritionist to offer a "Healthy Living Starter Pack."
- **Host events or webinars:** Partner with another business to host a free event or webinar that provides value to both of your audiences. This could be an educational session, a workshop, or even a fun community activity.
- **Share space or resources:** If you have a physical location, consider hosting a pop-up shop for another business, or share advertising space, such as newsletters or flyers.

Tap into free educational resources

Attend Webinars, Podcasts, and Workshops

- **Webinars:** Many organizations, including platforms like SCORE and the Small Business Administration (SBA), host free webinars on topics like marketing, financial management, and customer acquisition. These are often led by experienced professionals and provide practical, step-by-step advice.
- **Podcasts:** Subscribe to business-focused podcasts that align with your interests or industry. Popular options like *How I Built This, Smart Passive Income,* or *The Side Hustle School* feature interviews and tips from successful entrepreneurs.
- **Workshops and meetups:** Local workshops or virtual events can provide hands-on training and networking opportunities. Look for free events hosted by community

groups, libraries, or business associations.

Utilize Free Tools From Platforms Like SCORE or SBA

- **SCORE:** This nonprofit organization offers free one-on-one mentoring, webinars, templates, and guides on everything from business planning to marketing. Their mentors are often experienced business professionals who provide personalized advice.
- **Small Business Administration (SBA):** The SBA provides free online courses, articles, and tools tailored for entrepreneurs. You'll also find templates for business plans, financial projections, and other essential documents.
- **Local business development centers:** Many cities have Small Business Development Centers (SBDCs) that offer free consulting, training programs, and resources for startups.

Read Books and Case Studies on Successful Entrepreneurs

- **Business books:** Look for titles that focus on lean startups, entrepreneurship, and personal growth. Libraries often carry popular books for free, or you can check out digital options like Kindle Unlimited or Libby.
- **Case studies:** Many business blogs, university websites, and platforms like Harvard Business Review share detailed case studies on how businesses overcame challenges or achieved success.
- **Autobiographies and biographies:** Books like *Shoe Dog* by Phil Knight or *The Lean Startup* by Eric Ries offer firsthand insights into the entrepreneurial journey.

Build a support network

Join Entrepreneur or Small Business Groups

- **Online communities:** Platforms like Facebook, LinkedIn, and Reddit host groups tailored to entrepreneurs in various industries. Look for groups that align with your niche, goals, or geographic location.
- **Local meetups and organizations:** Attend events hosted by chambers of commerce, local coworking spaces, or business incubators. Networking events, workshops, and small business fairs are great opportunities to connect in person.
- **Industry-specific associations:** Many industries have associations or clubs that offer networking opportunities, resources, and support for small business owners.

Find Mentors Who've Succeeded on a Budget

- **Reach out through SCORE or similar programs:** Organizations like SCORE connect entrepreneurs with experienced mentors who volunteer their time to provide guidance.
- **Leverage your network:** Ask friends, family, or colleagues if they know someone with entrepreneurial experience who would be willing to mentor you.
- **Engage on social platforms:** LinkedIn is a great place to find and connect with professionals in your field. Send a polite message explaining why you admire their work and ask if they'd be open to offering advice.
- **Look for informal mentors:** Mentors don't always have

to be official. Even casual conversations with experienced business owners can provide valuable insights.

Collaborate With Peers for Shared Resources

- **Pool resources:** Share costs for things like advertising, event booths, or equipment rental with other small businesses in your area.
- **Swap services or skills:** Offer your expertise in exchange for services you need. For example, a graphic designer could trade branding services with a copywriter.
- **Promote each other:** Cross-promote with complementary businesses through social media, newsletters, or joint events. For example, a florist and a bakery could collaborate on wedding packages.
- **Create accountability groups:** Join or form a small group of peers to discuss goals, share challenges, and keep each other motivated.

Running Operations on a Shoestring Budget

Streamline operational costs

Use Virtual Tools for Remote Work

- Communication: Platforms like Zoom, Google Meet, and Slack make it easy to collaborate with team members, clients, or contractors in real time.
- Project management: Tools like Trello, Asana, or Monday.com help you track tasks, set deadlines, and organize projects efficiently.
- Cloud storage: Services like Google Drive or Dropbox allow you to store and share files securely without investing in physical storage solutions.
- Free or low-cost software: Look for free alternatives to expensive software. For example, Canva can replace advanced design software for basic needs, and Wave offers free accounting tools for small businesses.

Outsource Tasks to Freelancers or Interns

- **Hire freelancers for specialized tasks:** Platforms like Upwork, Fiverr, and Toptal connect you with talented professionals for tasks such as graphic design, content creation, or website development.
- **Offer internships:** Partner with local universities or career centers to find interns looking for experience in exchange for mentorship or college credit. This can be a cost-effective way to get help while giving back.
- **Outsource administrative tasks:** Virtual assistants can handle tasks like email management, scheduling, and data

entry, freeing you up to focus on strategic priorities.

Automate Repetitive Tasks Wherever Possible

- **Email marketing:** Use platforms like Mailchimp or Hub-Spot to automate email campaigns, nurture leads, and keep customers engaged.
- **Social media scheduling:** Tools like Hootsuite or Buffer allow you to plan and schedule posts in advance, saving you time on daily updates.
- **Customer relationship management (CRM):** CRMs like Zoho or HubSpot help you track interactions with customers, automate follow-ups, and manage sales pipelines.
- **Invoicing and payments:** Automate recurring invoices and payment reminders with tools like QuickBooks or Stripe.

Focus on high-impact, low-cost marketing

Launch an Email List for Direct Communication

- Choose an email marketing platform: Start with beginner-friendly tools like Mailchimp, ConvertKit, or Substack. Many offer free plans for small lists.
- Create a lead magnet: Offer a free resource—like an ebook, discount code, or checklist—in exchange for email sign-ups.
- Promote sign-ups everywhere: Add opt-in forms to your website, social media profiles, and blog posts.
- Engage your audience: Send regular emails with valuable content, updates, and special offers. Aim to educate and

entertain, not just sell.

Use Referral or Loyalty Programs to Build Customers

- **Referral incentives:** Offer discounts, free products, or other perks to customers who refer friends. For example, "Refer a friend and both get 10% off your next purchase."
- **Loyalty rewards:** Implement a points-based system where customers earn rewards for repeat purchases or actions like leaving reviews.
- **Easy sharing:** Provide tools like shareable links or codes that make it simple for customers to refer others.
- **Track and adjust:** Use tools like Yotpo or Smile.io to manage referral and loyalty programs efficiently.

Leverage Content Marketing Through Blogs and Videos

- **Start a blog:** Write posts that address common questions, offer tips, or share insights relevant to your target audience. Use free tools like WordPress or Medium to get started.
- **Create videos:** Short, engaging videos perform well on platforms like YouTube, Instagram, or TikTok. Use them to demonstrate products, share behind-the-scenes content, or explain how your business solves a problem.
- **Focus on SEO:** Use keywords that your target audience searches for to optimize your content for visibility. Free tools like Google Keyword Planner or Ubersuggest can help.
- **Be consistent:** Publish regularly to keep your audience engaged and grow your online presence over time.

Measure results with free analytics tools

Monitor Website Traffic and Engagement

Tools to use:

- **Google Analytics:** This free tool provides detailed insights into website traffic, user demographics, and behavior. You can track metrics like page views, bounce rates, and time spent on site.
- **Google Search Console:** Complement your analytics with search performance data, such as search terms that drive traffic and website errors that need fixing.

What to track:

- **Traffic sources:** Where are your visitors coming from—search engines, social media, or direct visits?
- **Popular pages:** Which pages attract the most views and keep users engaged?
- **User behavior:** Are visitors completing key actions, such as signing up for your email list or making purchases?

Track Social Media Performance

Tools to use:

- **Built-in platform analytics:** Platforms like Facebook, Instagram, LinkedIn, and Twitter provide free analytics dashboards to track engagement, reach, and follower growth.

- **Buffer or Hootsuite (free plans):** These tools allow you to monitor performance across multiple social platforms in one place.

What to track:

- **Engagement:** Which posts are receiving the most likes, comments, and shares?
- **Reach:** How many people are seeing your content?
- **Audience growth:** Are your follower counts increasing over time?

Analyze Customer Behavior for Improvement

Tools to use:

- **CRM platforms:** Free or low-cost options like HubSpot or Zoho CRM provide insights into customer interactions and buying behavior.
- **Email marketing tools:** Platforms like Mailchimp or ConvertKit show open rates, click-through rates, and the success of your campaigns.
- **Heatmaps and session recording tools:** Free versions of tools like Hotjar or Crazy Egg let you see how users navigate your website.

What to track:

- **Purchase patterns:** What products or services are most popular?
- **Feedback trends:** What common themes emerge in

reviews or surveys?

- **Engagement habits:** When and how are customers interacting with your business?

Using this data, you can tweak your offerings, improve your messaging, and create a more customer-focused experience.

Marketing Magic: Attracting Customers Without Breaking the Bank

Building a strong brand is essential for differentiating your business and connecting with your audience, but you don't need a massive budget to get started. By defining your brand identity and staying consistent across all touchpoints, you can create a memorable and impactful brand that resonates with your target market.

Building Your Brand on a Budget

Define your brand identity

1. Create a Memorable Logo and Tagline

- **Use free design tools:** Platforms like Canva and Looka offer free logo-making tools with easy-to-use templates. Even if you're not a designer, you can create a professional-looking logo in minutes.
- **Keep it simple:** Aim for a clean and simple design that's easy to recognize and reproduce. Avoid overly complex graphics that may not scale well across different mediums.
- **Incorporate your brand values:** Think about what you

want your logo to communicate. Does it reflect your business's mission, personality, and style?

Crafting your tagline:

- **Make it memorable:** A good tagline is short, catchy, and to the point. It should communicate what your business does and why it matters.
- **Use free tools for inspiration:** Look to websites like Shopify's slogan maker or HubSpot's free tagline generator for creative ideas.

2. Develop a Consistent Tone and Visual Style

Tone of voice:

- **Know your audience:** Are they professional and corporate, or do they prefer a more casual, friendly tone? Tailor your messaging accordingly.
- **Be consistent:** Whether it's your website copy, social media posts, or customer emails, ensure the tone remains the same across all platforms.
- **Use free resources:** Platforms like Grammarly can help ensure your tone is clear and consistent in written content.

Visual style:

- **Color palette:** Choose 2-3 colors that reflect your brand's personality. For example, blue might communicate trust, while yellow could evoke energy and optimism.
- **Typography:** Select fonts that are readable and align with

your brand's vibe. Keep it simple with one or two font choices for consistency.

- **Free design tools:** Canva, again, is an excellent resource for creating consistent visual content. It offers templates for everything from social media posts to flyers, helping you maintain a cohesive visual identity across all channels.

3. Align Branding with Your Target Audience's Preferences

- **Conduct audience research:** Use surveys, social media polls, or simple conversations with your customers to understand their pain points, motivations, and preferences.
- **Analyze competitors:** Look at how other businesses in your industry present their brands. What works well? What could be improved? Use this information to carve out your own niche.
- **Tailor your message:** Ensure that your branding speaks to your audience's desires. If your customers value sustainability, for example, make sure that comes through in your logo, tagline, and overall messaging.

Establish an online presence

1. Build a Professional Website with Low-Cost Platforms

- **Wix:** Known for its drag-and-drop interface, Wix offers a variety of customizable templates for businesses on a budget. You can start for free and scale up as needed.
- **Squarespace:** With a clean, modern design and a user-friendly editor, Squarespace is ideal for creating visually appealing websites without the need for coding.

- **WordPress:** If you're a bit more tech-savvy, WordPress offers a flexible platform for creating and customizing websites. Many hosting providers offer affordable WordPress plans.

2. Optimize Your Site for Mobile and SEO

Mobile optimization:

- **Responsive design:** Make sure your website automatically adjusts to fit various screen sizes. Most website builders, like Wix and Squarespace, offer responsive design templates that work on both desktop and mobile devices.
- **Fast load times:** Mobile users tend to abandon websites that take too long to load, so ensure your images are optimized and your site runs smoothly. Tools like Google PageSpeed Insights can help you check and improve load times.

Search Engine Optimization (SEO):

- **Keyword research:** Use free tools like Google Keyword Planner to find the best keywords for your business and incorporate them into your website content.
- **Optimize your content:** Include relevant keywords in your headings, meta descriptions, and alt text for images.
- **Create valuable content:** Google favors websites that offer high-quality, informative content. Adding a blog or resource page to your site can help you rank higher in search results.

3. Create Business Profiles on Major Social Media Platforms

- **Facebook:** Create a business page where you can share updates, promotions, and engage with your community. Facebook also offers advertising options to expand your reach.
- **Instagram:** Perfect for visually-driven businesses, Instagram allows you to showcase your products or services through photos and stories.
- **LinkedIn:** If you're in a B2B space, LinkedIn is ideal for connecting with other professionals, sharing thought leadership content, and building relationships.
- **TikTok:** For businesses targeting younger audiences, TikTok's short-form video format can help you build brand awareness in a fun and engaging way.

Tips for setting up your profiles:

- **Consistent branding:** Use the same logo, color scheme, and tone across all your social media platforms to reinforce your brand identity.
- **Complete your profiles:** Make sure to fill out all relevant details, including contact information, website links, and a compelling bio that describes your business.
- **Post regularly:** Aim to post consistently to keep your audience engaged and build a loyal following. Use social media management tools like Buffer or Hootsuite to schedule posts in advance.

Leverage storytelling to connect with customers

1. Share Your "Why" Through Personal Stories

How to share your story:

- **Be authentic:** Customers appreciate transparency and honesty. Share your motivations, challenges, and triumphs in a way that feels real and relatable.
- **Focus on the journey:** Explain how your experiences led you to launch your business. Maybe it was a personal struggle, a passion for solving a particular problem, or a desire to make a difference.
- **Humanize your brand:** Show the person behind the business. When customers feel like they know you on a deeper level, they're more likely to trust you and engage with your brand.

Example:

If you launched your business to provide a solution to a personal pain point, tell that story. Maybe your struggle with finding affordable, high-quality products inspired you to create your own. By sharing that journey, you make your business more relatable and approachable.

2. Use Customer Testimonials or Case Studies

How to use testimonials effectively:

- **Gather real feedback:** Ask your satisfied customers to

share their experiences with your business. Use platforms like email, social media, or even Google reviews to collect these testimonials.

- **Show results:** Case studies and testimonials that demonstrate specific results (for example, "I saved X amount of money" or "This service helped me achieve Y") are particularly impactful.
- **Highlight emotions:** A good testimonial tells a story of how your product or service improved the customer's life. Focus on the emotions behind their experience, not just the features of your product.

Example:

A customer who used your budget-friendly business tools could share how your solution helped them start their own successful venture on a tight budget. When potential customers read these stories, they can see themselves achieving similar results.

3. Create Content That Highlights Your Unique Journey

How to share your journey effectively:

- **Behind-the-scenes content:** Show what goes on behind the scenes of your business. Whether it's the challenges you face, the successes you celebrate, or the lessons you learn along the way, letting your audience in on your journey builds a sense of community.
- **Share milestones and setbacks:** Business journeys are rarely smooth, and people appreciate the honesty that comes with sharing both the highs and lows. Don't be afraid

to talk about your challenges—just be sure to highlight how you've overcome them.

- **Engage with your audience:** Ask your followers for their feedback, questions, or stories. Involve them in your journey, making them feel like they're a part of your success.

Example:

Documenting your business's growth from a small idea to a full-fledged operation is a great way to inspire your audience. Share posts about your initial struggles, how you found solutions, and the growth you've experienced. As people see your brand evolve, they feel more connected to your success.

Low-Cost Marketing Strategies That Work

Use social media to grow your reach

1. Post Engaging Content Regularly

Types of engaging content to post:

- **Educational posts:** Share tips, how-tos, and insights that offer value to your audience. Whether it's a business tip, product tutorial, or industry news, educational content positions you as an expert in your field.
- **Behind-the-scenes content:** Give followers a glimpse into your daily business operations, show them your team, or document your process. People love seeing the human side of a business!
- **User-generated content:** Encourage customers to share photos, videos, or stories about their experience with your product or service. Reposting this content not only helps build credibility but also makes your customers feel valued.
- **Polls and questions:** Engage directly with your audience by asking for their opinions or feedback. Use polls or questions in your posts or stories to spark conversation and learn more about your audience's preferences.

Tools to schedule posts:

- **Buffer:** Schedule posts in advance to maintain consistency.
- **Later:** Plan and schedule visual content to maintain a consistent aesthetic.

2. Interact with Followers to Build Trust and Community

- **Respond to comments and messages:** Take the time to reply to comments on your posts and direct messages. Whether it's a question or a compliment, your followers will appreciate the personal touch.
- **Like and comment on followers' posts:** Interacting with your followers' content shows that you care about them, not just their business with you. It helps you build a community where your audience feels seen and heard.
- **Host live sessions:** Live videos are a great way to engage with your audience in real time. You can answer questions, showcase new products, or host Q&A sessions to deepen your connection with followers.
- **Create a sense of belonging:** Use inclusive language and create posts that resonate with your community's interests. The more you make your audience feel like they're part of something, the more loyal they'll become.

3. Collaborate with Influencers or Micro-Influencers

- **Identify relevant influencers:** Look for influencers whose audience aligns with your target market. They don't need to have millions of followers—micro-influencers (1k-100k followers) can offer high engagement rates and niche audiences.
- **Offer value:** Be clear about what both you and the influencer will gain from the partnership. You can offer free products, a monetary incentive, or a shoutout in exchange for the influencer promoting your business.
- **Create authentic partnerships:** Authenticity is key in influencer collaborations. Choose influencers who genuinely resonate with your brand and values. Their endorsement

will feel more genuine and therefore more impactful to their audience.

Example:

If you sell handmade jewelry, find a micro-influencer in the fashion or lifestyle space who aligns with your brand's aesthetic. A collaboration could include them wearing your pieces in a post, tagging your business, and sharing a special discount code with their followers.

Harness the power of content marketing

1. Write Blog Posts or Create Videos Answering FAQs

- **Identify common questions:** Start by compiling a list of questions you get from customers or ones related to your industry. You can also use online forums, social media, and Google search suggestions to find out what people are asking.
- **Write helpful blog posts:** Write detailed, informative posts that directly answer those questions. Use clear, simple language, and structure your content for easy reading (headings, bullet points, etc.).
- **Create short videos:** Video content is highly engaging, so consider creating short videos that answer FAQs. These can be shared on social media, YouTube, or embedded on your website. People often prefer watching videos over reading, so videos are a great way to boost engagement.

2. Develop Free Resources (Guides or Templates) to Attract Leads

Types of free resources to create:

- **E-books or guides:** Write in-depth guides on a topic related to your business. For example, if you run a digital marketing service, create a guide titled "How to Build an Effective Social Media Strategy for Small Businesses."
- **Templates:** Offer downloadable templates that make tasks easier for your audience. A simple but useful template like a "Budget Planning Template" can attract leads who may later become customers.
- **Checklists and toolkits:** People love easy-to-use resources. Create checklists or toolkits that help them complete a task more efficiently. For instance, a "Startup Checklist for New Entrepreneurs" could be incredibly valuable to your audience.

How to promote your free resources:

- **Use landing pages:** Create a dedicated landing page where visitors can download your free resource in exchange for their email address.
- **Share on social media:** Promote your free resources across your social media channels to increase exposure.
- **Offer incentives:** Provide an incentive, like a discount on your products or services, to encourage people to download your resources.

3. Use Repurposed Content Across Multiple Platforms

- **Blog post to social media:** Turn a blog post into a series of social media posts. Break down the main points, add a quote or image, and post them over several days or weeks.
- **Videos to blog posts or podcasts:** If you create a video, consider transcribing it and turning it into a blog post. Or, repurpose the video as a podcast episode for those who prefer audio content.
- **Create an infographic:** Summarize key takeaways from a blog post or video in an eye-catching infographic that can be shared on social media or your website.
- **Email newsletters:** Include summaries or highlights of your blog posts and videos in your email newsletters to drive more traffic back to your content.

Focus on word-of-mouth and referrals

1. Encourage Satisfied Customers to Spread the Word

- **Ask for reviews:** After a purchase or service, ask your happy customers to leave a review or testimonial. Make it easy for them by providing links to review sites (Google, Yelp, Trustpilot).
- **Request referrals:** Don't be shy about asking customers to refer friends or colleagues who might benefit from your products or services.
- **Provide shareable content:** Create content that's easy for your customers to share. This could be a blog post, an infographic, or a special offer they can forward to others.
- **Show appreciation:** Make sure to thank customers who refer others to your business. People are more likely to refer when they feel valued.

2. Offer Incentives Like Discounts or Free Trials for Referrals

- **Discounts on future purchases:** Offer a percentage off a future order or service when customers refer a friend. For example, "Refer a friend and get 20% off your next purchase."
- **Free trials or upgrades:** Offer free trials of a new service or product to customers who refer others. This works especially well if you have subscription-based products or services.
- **Exclusive rewards:** Create a tiered referral program where customers earn more significant rewards after referring multiple people. This could include exclusive products, free services, or VIP status.

3. Partner with Complementary Businesses for Mutual Promotion

- **Find the right partners:** Look for businesses that share your target audience but are not direct competitors. For example, if you sell handmade candles, you could partner with a local artisan soap maker.
- **Create joint promotions:** Collaborate on special offers, bundles, or events that encourage both of your customers to check out the other business. For example, you could offer a discount on each other's products when customers purchase from both businesses.
- **Co-host events or webinars:** Partner with another business to host a joint event or webinar that adds value to your audience. This could be an online workshop or an

in-person event.

- **Social media shout-outs:** Give each other a shout-out on social media, introducing your followers to your partner's business. This can help both of you gain new followers and build a broader customer base.

Measuring Marketing Success

Set clear marketing goals

1. Define Specific Targets for Customer Acquisition

- **Identify your ideal customer:** Create customer personas based on your target audience's demographics, behaviors, and pain points. The more specific you are about who you're trying to reach, the better your marketing efforts will be.

- **Set quantitative goals:** Define how many new customers you want to acquire in a set period. For example, "I want to acquire 100 new customers this quarter."
- **Consider acquisition channels:** Determine where your customers are most likely to come from. Will they find you through social media, paid ads, or word-of-mouth referrals? Knowing this helps you focus on the right marketing channels.

2. Create Timelines for Achieving Milestones

- **Start with short-term goals:** Break your larger target into smaller, manageable steps. For example, if you want to acquire 100 new customers in three months, aim to gain around 30 new customers each month.
- **Assign deadlines:** Set deadlines for each milestone to create urgency and stay focused. For example, "Complete a social media campaign by the end of the month to acquire 25 new leads."
- **Review and adjust:** Regularly review your progress and adjust your strategy if needed. If a particular tactic isn't working, don't be afraid to tweak your plan or try a different approach.

3. Focus on One or Two Key Metrics at a Time

- **Identify your top priorities:** Depending on your marketing goals, choose metrics that directly align with your objectives. If customer acquisition is your goal, focus on metrics like the number of new leads or conversion rates.

- **Track ROI:** Focus on metrics that show the return on investment (ROI) for your marketing efforts. For example, track the cost per acquisition (CPA) or the lifetime value (LTV) of customers.
- **Use tools to track performance:** Use analytics tools like Google Analytics, social media insights, or email marketing platforms to track and measure your chosen metrics.

Use free or inexpensive tracking tools

1. Monitor Website Traffic with Google Analytics

How to use Google Analytics for tracking website traffic:

- **Set up tracking codes:** First, you'll need to add a small tracking code to your website to start collecting data. Google Analytics provides clear instructions on how to do this.
- **Monitor key metrics:** Focus on key metrics like page views, bounce rate, average session duration, and traffic sources. These indicators will help you understand how visitors are finding and engaging with your site.
- **Set goals:** Google Analytics allows you to set up specific goals, like completing a purchase or filling out a contact form. This helps you track conversion rates and measure how well your website is achieving your business objectives.
- **Use reports:** Take advantage of Google Analytics' various reports, including audience demographics, user behavior, and acquisition channels, to get a deeper understanding of

your website's performance.

2. Track Email Marketing Performance with Free Tools Like Mailchimp

- **Track open rates and click-through rates (CTR):** These are two of the most important metrics to gauge the success of your email campaigns. Open rates show how many people are reading your emails, while CTR indicates how many are clicking through to your website or offer.
- **Measure conversion rates:** Use Mailchimp's e-commerce integration (if applicable) to track how many subscribers are converting into customers after clicking on your emails.
- **A/B testing:** Mailchimp offers A/B testing for free, allowing you to test different subject lines, content, or images to see which variations perform better.
- **Segmentation:** With Mailchimp, you can segment your email list to tailor your messaging. Track how different segments respond to your campaigns and adjust your approach for better results.

3. Use Social Media Analytics to Evaluate Engagement

- **Track engagement metrics:** Look at likes, shares, comments, and other interactions to gauge how well your content is resonating with your audience. Engagement metrics give you a good sense of which posts are driving the most interest.
- **Analyze audience demographics:** Social media platforms offer insights into your audience's demographics, such as age, gender, location, and interests. This information

allows you to tailor your content to better meet the needs of your target audience.

- **Measure growth:** Keep an eye on your follower count, reach, and impressions over time to see if your audience is growing. This can help you understand whether your social media efforts are paying off.
- **Monitor top-performing posts:** Identify the posts that are getting the most engagement and replicate their success. Whether it's a certain type of content or a particular posting time, recognizing patterns can help improve your future posts.

Adjust strategies based on data

1. Identify Which Campaigns Deliver the Best ROI

How to identify high-ROI campaigns:

- **Compare cost vs. return:** Evaluate how much you spent on each campaign and compare that to the revenue or leads it generated. For example, if you spent $500 on an ad campaign and earned $2,000 in sales, your ROI is strong.
- **Track conversion rates:** Focus on campaigns that lead to tangible actions, such as purchases, sign-ups, or other key conversions. High-conversion campaigns typically indicate strong ROI.
- **Use UTM parameters:** To track the effectiveness of specific campaigns or marketing channels, use UTM (Urchin Tracking Module) parameters. These tags help you identify which campaigns, social media posts, or emails are driving traffic and conversions.

2. Drop or Modify Underperforming Strategies

- **Analyze the data:** Look at metrics like engagement rates, conversion rates, and ROI to identify areas where your strategy may be falling short. For example, if a paid ad campaign is costing more than it's earning, it may need to be adjusted.
- **Refine your approach:** If something isn't working, don't necessarily abandon it—try tweaking it first. For example, if a social media ad isn't generating sales, experiment with different targeting, messaging, or creative.
- **Cut losses early:** If after making adjustments, a strategy is still underperforming, it might be time to cut your losses and redirect resources to more effective campaigns.

3. Experiment with New Approaches Based on Insights

- **A/B testing:** Run A/B tests on your campaigns to experiment with different versions of ads, email subject lines, landing pages, and more. Testing small changes helps you identify which elements work best.
- **Test new channels:** If your current marketing channels are delivering mediocre results, try experimenting with new ones. For example, if social media isn't bringing in leads, consider experimenting with influencer partnerships or paid search.
- **Implement customer feedback:** Use insights from customer surveys, reviews, and feedback to shape your strategies. If customers are expressing interest in certain features or types of content, experiment with incorporating those into your campaigns.

- **Innovate with content:** If your blog posts are performing well, consider expanding into other forms of content, such as video or podcasts, to see how your audience reacts.

Marketing is not a one-size-fits-all approach, and being open to adjusting strategies is crucial for sustained growth. By identifying which campaigns are delivering the best ROI, modifying or dropping underperforming strategies, and experimenting with new approaches based on data insights, you can optimize your marketing efforts and achieve better results.

The key is to stay data-driven and remain flexible—tweaking and evolving your strategies as you gather more information. By embracing this approach, you'll be able to build a marketing plan that not only works but continues to improve over time, helping your business grow and thrive.

Scaling Smartly: Growing Without Overspending

As your business grows, expanding your customer base is essential for long-term success. Tapping into new markets allows you to reach more potential customers and diversify your revenue streams. However, entering a new market requires thoughtful strategy and careful testing to ensure your efforts are cost-effective. Here's how to successfully expand your customer base by identifying new opportunities and testing them with minimal risk.

Expanding Your Customer Base

Tap into new markets

1. Identify Adjacent Niches or Underserved Customer Segments

- **Look at customer behavior:** Analyze your existing customer data to identify trends or patterns that could point to new opportunities. For example, if you sell fitness gear, you may find that parents of young children are interested in quick workouts at home—an underserved market within your niche.
- **Research competitors:** Study your competitors and look for areas where they may not be fully addressing certain customer needs. If you can offer a product or service that fills this gap, you could capture a significant share of that underserved market.
- **Survey your current customers:** Ask your existing customers if they have any unmet needs or if there are related products or services they wish you offered. This feedback can help you identify new opportunities to serve them better.

2. Customize Offerings for Specific Groups

- **Adapt product features or pricing:** If you're targeting a new demographic, consider adjusting your product features or pricing to better suit their needs. For example, if you're targeting a younger audience, you may want to offer more budget-friendly options or smaller-sized packages.
- **Create targeted marketing messages:** Develop tailored messaging that speaks directly to the needs and desires

of the specific customer segments. Highlight the unique benefits your product or service offers to that group.

- **Offer bundles or packages:** Group complementary products together in bundles to appeal to different segments. For example, if you sell skincare products, create bundles specifically for dry skin or anti-aging to cater to customers with specific needs.

3. Test New Markets with Low-Cost Campaigns

- **Start with small, targeted ads:** Use low-budget social media ads to target specific customer segments in the new market. This allows you to gauge interest without a large upfront investment.
- **Run A/B tests:** Test different versions of your product offerings, messaging, or ads to see which approach works best with your new audience. A/B testing lets you experiment with minimal risk.
- **Leverage email marketing:** If you have an email list with relevant contacts, use it to run segmented campaigns targeting new groups. This can be a cost-effective way to test new products or messaging in a targeted way.
- **Offer special promotions:** Launch limited-time offers or discounts to attract attention from the new market. This can help generate buzz and encourage early adoption without a significant investment.

Build long-term customer relationships

1. Use Email Marketing to Nurture Repeat Buyers

- **Create a welcome series:** Start with a warm and engaging email series for new customers. Share your story, thank them for their purchase, and provide helpful tips related to your products or services.
- **Send exclusive offers:** Reward loyal customers with special discounts or early access to sales. Make them feel appreciated for their ongoing support.
- **Share useful content:** Provide educational or entertaining content that aligns with their interests. For instance, if you sell gardening tools, share seasonal planting tips or DIY guides.
- **Stay consistent:** Regularly communicate with your customers through a well-planned schedule, but avoid overwhelming them with too many emails.

2. Personalize Interactions to Make Customers Feel Valued

- **Use customer data:** Leverage purchase history, browsing behavior, or survey responses to tailor your communication. For example, recommend products based on their previous purchases.
- **Address customers by name:** Whether it's in an email, social media message, or customer service interaction, using a customer's name adds a personal touch.
- **Acknowledge milestones:** Celebrate customer birthdays, anniversaries, or other special moments with personalized messages or offers.

- **Respond promptly:** Quick and friendly responses to inquiries or feedback show customers that you care about their experience.

3. Offer Exceptional Customer Service as a Competitive Edge

- **Be proactive:** Anticipate customer needs and address potential issues before they arise. For example, send follow-up emails to ensure they're satisfied with their purchase.
- **Solve problems quickly:** When customers encounter an issue, resolve it promptly and with a positive attitude. Offer solutions that go above and beyond expectations.
- **Create a feedback loop:** Encourage customers to share their thoughts and suggestions. Act on their feedback to show that you value their input.
- **Train your team:** If you have employees or contractors, ensure they're well-trained in providing outstanding customer service that reflects your brand values.

Create customer loyalty programs

1. Design a Points-Based Rewards System

- **Set clear rules:** Make it easy for customers to understand how they can earn and redeem points. For example, offer 1 point for every $1 spent, with 100 points redeemable for a discount or free product.
- **Include bonus opportunities:** Encourage engagement by offering bonus points for specific actions, such as referring a friend, leaving a review, or making a purchase during a

promotional period.

- **Use digital tools:** Implement an affordable loyalty app or integrate rewards tracking into your online store to simplify the process for you and your customers.

2. Offer Exclusive Perks for Repeat Customers

Ideas for exclusive perks:

- **Early access to sales or new products:** Let your loyal customers be the first to shop during major sales or try new offerings.
- **Personalized gifts or thank-you notes:** Surprise your top customers with a small token of appreciation, such as a free sample, exclusive content, or a handwritten note.
- **Members-only events:** Host virtual or in-person events exclusively for your most loyal customers, such as product demos, workshops, or Q&A sessions.

3. Use Feedback to Improve Loyalty Incentives

- **Survey your customers:** Ask your audience what types of rewards or perks they'd find most valuable. You can do this through email surveys, social media polls, or one-on-one conversations.
- **Analyze participation rates:** If certain rewards or features aren't being used, consider phasing them out in favor of more popular options.
- **Test new ideas:** Experiment with different rewards or incentives based on customer suggestions, and monitor their impact on engagement and sales.

Scaling Operations Efficiently

Streamline processes for growth

1. Document Workflows to Ensure Consistency

- **Break down each process step-by-step:** Identify the key tasks involved in your daily operations, such as managing orders, responding to customer inquiries, or tracking inventory.
- **Create clear instructions:** Use concise language and visuals like flowcharts, checklists, or video tutorials to make your workflows easy to understand.
- **Standardize processes:** Ensure everyone follows the same procedures to deliver a consistent experience to your customers.
- **Review and update regularly:** As your business evolves, revisit your workflows to reflect changes or improvements.

91

2. Automate Administrative Tasks to Save Time

- **Email marketing:** Use tools like Mailchimp or ConvertKit to schedule and send automated email campaigns.
- **Social media scheduling:** Platforms like Buffer or Hootsuite allow you to plan and publish posts in advance.
- **Invoicing and payments:** Apps like QuickBooks or Wave automate billing, payment reminders, and financial tracking.
- **Customer support:** Chatbots or automated FAQ pages can handle common inquiries, leaving you more time to address complex issues.

3. Delegate or Outsource Time-Intensive Responsibilities

- **Identify tasks to offload:** Look for time-consuming or specialized tasks, such as graphic design, content creation, or bookkeeping.
- **Hire freelancers or contractors:** Platforms like Upwork, Fiverr, or local networks can connect you with skilled professionals for affordable rates.
- **Train team members:** If you have a small team, invest time in training them to handle key responsibilities.
- **Start small:** Begin with one or two tasks and gradually expand as you gain confidence in the delegation process.

Manage costs as you scale

1. Monitor Expenses Carefully to Avoid Overspending

- **Use accounting software:** Tools like QuickBooks, Wave,

or Xero can help you track your income and expenses in real time.

- **Create a budget:** Establish a detailed budget for each area of your business, such as marketing, operations, and inventory.
- **Review regularly:** Schedule monthly or quarterly reviews of your financial statements to identify trends, flag unnecessary spending, and adjust as needed.
- **Avoid impulse purchases:** Before making a significant investment, assess whether it aligns with your long-term goals and current budget.

2. Focus on Reinvesting Profits for Strategic Growth

Where to reinvest profits:

- **Marketing and customer acquisition:** Allocate funds to high-impact campaigns that attract new customers and drive sales.
- **Technology and tools:** Invest in software, equipment, or automation tools that improve efficiency and reduce costs over time.
- **Product development:** Expand your offerings by introducing new products or enhancing existing ones based on customer feedback.
- **Team building:** Hire skilled employees or freelancers to take on specialized tasks and support your growth.

3. Negotiate Better Deals with Vendors or Suppliers

Tips for negotiating effectively:

- **Highlight your growing volume:** If you're ordering more frequently or in larger quantities, use this as a bargaining chip to request discounts.
- **Compare options:** Get quotes from multiple suppliers to ensure you're getting the best deal.
- **Ask for flexible terms:** Negotiate payment schedules, bulk discounts, or reduced shipping costs to improve cash flow.
- **Build strong relationships:** Establish a good rapport with your suppliers by being reliable and communicative—it can make them more willing to accommodate your needs.

Hire smartly without breaking the bank

1. Start with Freelancers or Part-Time Help

Benefits of hiring freelancers or part-time help:

- **Cost efficiency:** You pay for specific tasks or hours worked, avoiding the costs of full-time salaries, benefits, and taxes.
- **Scalability:** Freelancers can help with short-term projects or seasonal surges in demand, allowing you to adjust your workforce as needed.
- **Access to specialized skills:** Freelancers often bring expertise in areas like graphic design, marketing, or web development, which may not require a full-time employee.

Where to start: Identify tasks that can be outsourced and look for freelancers or part-time workers to handle them, freeing up your time to focus on core business activities.

2. Use Online Platforms to Find Skilled Workers Affordably

- **Freelancing websites:** Sites like Upwork, Fiverr, and Toptal connect you with freelancers across various fields and budget ranges.
- **Remote job boards:** Platforms like We Work Remotely or FlexJobs are great for finding remote workers interested in part-time or project-based roles.
- **Local networks:** Check community forums, Facebook groups, or LinkedIn for skilled professionals in your area who may be looking for flexible work opportunities.

3. Offer Non-Monetary Incentives to Attract Talent

Creative incentives to consider:

- **Flexible work arrangements:** Allowing remote work or flexible hours can appeal to workers seeking better work-life balance.
- **Skill-building opportunities:** Offer access to training, courses, or certifications that help workers grow professionally.
- **Recognition and growth:** Provide a clear path for advancement and recognize contributions through public appreciation or small awards.
- **Equity or profit-sharing:** For key roles, consider offering a stake in the company's success as an alternative to a high salary.

Diversifying Revenue Streams

Add complementary products or services

1. Identify Offerings That Align with Your Existing Niche

How to identify complementary offerings:

- **Listen to customer feedback:** Pay attention to what your customers are asking for or what challenges they face related to your current offerings.
- **Analyze your industry:** Look at successful businesses in your niche and see what complementary products or services they provide.

- **Focus on solving problems:** Think about additional ways you can address your customers' pain points or enhance their experience with your brand.

For example, if you sell fitness equipment, you might add workout plans or nutritional guides as complementary services.

2. Test New Ideas Through Pilot Programs or Surveys

Steps to test new offerings:

- **Conduct surveys:** Ask your existing customers for their input on potential additions. Use tools like Google Forms or SurveyMonkey to gather feedback.
- **Run a pilot program:** Launch a limited version of your new product or service to a small group and collect feedback on its value and usability.
- **Use A/B testing:** If you're offering new digital services, test different versions to see which resonates most with your audience.

3. Bundle Products or Services for Higher Value

How to create effective bundles:

- **Focus on synergy:** Combine offerings that naturally go together, such as pairing a product with a service or bundling related products.
- **Offer discounts or incentives:** Provide a slight price reduction for bundled packages to make them more attractive than purchasing items individually.

- **Highlight the benefits:** Clearly communicate the added value customers receive by purchasing the bundle.

For example, a photography business could bundle a photoshoot session with editing services and digital prints at a discounted rate.

Explore digital revenue opportunities

1. Create Online Courses, eBooks, or Subscription Services

Steps to create digital products:

- **Identify a niche topic:** Focus on areas where you have expertise and that address a specific need or problem for your audience.
- **Develop high-quality content:** Use accessible tools like Canva for eBooks, Teachable or Udemy for courses, and Patreon or Substack for subscription services.
- **Market your product:** Use your website, social media, and email lists to promote your offerings and build excitement around your launch.

For example, a business consultant could create an online course on budgeting for startups or an eBook on writing lean business plans.

2. Monetize Content Through Affiliate Marketing

- **Join affiliate programs:** Sign up for programs like Amazon Associates, ShareASale, or those offered by niche brands in your industry.
- **Create content around products:** Write blogs, make videos, or post on social media highlighting the benefits of the products you recommend.
- **Include affiliate links:** Share your unique affiliate links, earning a commission whenever someone makes a purchase through your link.

3. Sell on E-Commerce Platforms with Minimal Overhead

Steps to start selling on e-commerce platforms:

- **Choose the right platform:** Use marketplaces like Etsy for handmade goods, Gumroad for digital downloads, or Shopify for a dedicated store.
- **Focus on low-cost inventory:** Begin with a small inventory of high-demand products to minimize risk. Alternatively, use print-on-demand services to eliminate inventory costs.
- **Optimize listings:** Create clear, engaging product descriptions and use high-quality images to attract buyers.

Partner with other businesses

1. Cross-Promote Services with Complementary Brands

- **Identify complementary businesses:** Look for brands that serve a similar target market without directly competing with your products or services.

- **Share platforms:** Promote each other's offerings through email campaigns, social media shoutouts, or bundled packages.
- **Highlight mutual benefits:** Show customers how your combined offerings work together to meet their needs more effectively.

For example, a graphic designer could partner with a website developer to provide clients with a full suite of branding and online presence services.

2. Collaborate on Joint Ventures or Projects

Ideas for collaboration:

- **Co-host events:** Run workshops, webinars, or community events to showcase both brands while sharing the costs and effort.
- **Create bundled offers:** Develop special packages that combine your products or services with those of your partner business.
- **Launch joint marketing campaigns:** Share the cost of advertising while benefiting from increased exposure to each other's audiences.

3. Share Costs and Resources for Mutual Growth

Ways to share resources:

- **Split operational costs:** Share office space, equipment, or supplies to reduce overhead.

- **Collaborate on bulk purchases:** Order inventory together to take advantage of discounts.
- **Share expertise:** Trade services or knowledge to help each other grow without additional expenses.

For instance, a small bakery could partner with a coffee shop to share delivery costs or co-market their products.

Staying Profitable: Long-Term Success Strategies

Sound financial management is the backbone of any successful business, especially when you're working with a tight budget. By keeping track of income and expenses, separating personal and business finances, and preparing for taxes and unexpected costs, you can build a financially resilient business.

Managing Business Finances Effectively

Keep track of income and expenses

1. Use Budgeting Tools to Monitor Cash Flow

- **Use budgeting tools:** Free or low-cost tools like Wave, QuickBooks, or Excel templates can help you track income and expenses. There are also many free budget templates available on the internet.
- **Review finances regularly:** Set aside time weekly or monthly to review your cash flow and identify trends.
- **Plan for lean periods:** Anticipate slower seasons and adjust spending accordingly to maintain financial stability.

2. Separate Personal and Business Finances

Steps to separate finances:

- **Open a business bank account:** Use a dedicated account for all business transactions to streamline tracking and reporting.
- **Avoid mixing funds:** Pay yourself a set salary or draw instead of using business funds for personal expenses.
- **Use separate credit cards:** Apply for a business credit card to build business credit and keep expenses distinct.

<u>Important:</u> Clear separation simplifies bookkeeping and is vital for tax reporting and securing future funding.

3. Prepare for Taxes and Unforeseen Costs

How to stay prepared:

- **Set aside money for taxes:** Estimate your tax liability and save a percentage of your income to cover it. Tools like IRS or CRA calculators can help with accurate estimates.
- **Create an emergency fund:** Save a portion of your profits for unforeseen expenses like equipment repairs or unexpected opportunities.
- **Consult a professional:** Work with an accountant or tax advisor to ensure compliance and identify any potential deductions.

Focus on profitability, not just revenue

1. Identify High-Margin Products or Services

Steps to identify high-margin opportunities:

- **Analyze your current offerings:** Determine which products or services yield the highest profit relative to their cost.
- **Promote these offerings:** Prioritize marketing and sales efforts for your most profitable items.
- **Refine your pricing strategy:** Ensure your prices reflect the value provided while maintaining a healthy margin.

For example, if you're running a bakery, premium custom cakes might have a higher profit margin than basic bread loaves.

2. Cut Costs on Low-Value Activities

How to reduce unnecessary costs:

- **Assess all expenses:** Regularly review where your money is going and identify areas for cost-cutting.
- **Automate or streamline processes:** Use affordable tools to handle repetitive tasks more efficiently.
- **Focus on ROI:** Allocate resources only to activities that directly support profitability, such as customer acquisition or high-impact marketing.

3. Set Profit Benchmarks and Track Progress

How to set and track profit benchmarks:

- **Define measurable targets:** For example, aim for a specific profit margin percentage each month or quarter.
- **Monitor your performance:** Use accounting tools to regularly review your profit and loss statements.

- **Adjust as needed:** If benchmarks aren't being met, reassess your pricing, costs, or focus areas to realign with your goals.

Create a financial safety net

1. Build an Emergency Fund for Unexpected Challenges

How to build an emergency fund:

- **Set a savings goal:** Aim to save enough to cover at least three to six months of operating expenses.
- **Allocate a percentage of profits:** Regularly set aside a portion of your earnings into a separate account.
- **Start small and grow consistently:** Even modest contributions add up over time, providing a cushion when you need it most.

2. Diversify Revenue Streams for Stability

Ways to diversify your income:

- **Introduce complementary products or services:** For example, a fitness trainer might offer online classes or sell branded merchandise.
- **Explore passive income opportunities:** Consider options like affiliate marketing, digital products, or subscription services.
- **Serve different customer segments:** Tailor offerings to meet the needs of adjacent markets.

3. Regularly Review Financial Goals and Adjust Plans

- **Schedule financial check-ins:** Review your financial goals, income, and expenses monthly or quarterly.
- **Track key metrics:** Monitor profit margins, cash flow, and revenue growth to identify trends.
- **Adapt to changes:** Be flexible and ready to update your plans based on market conditions or unexpected opportunities.

Maintaining Momentum and Adapting to Change

Stay Ahead of Industry Needs

1. Monitor Competitors and Market Shifts

How to stay informed:

- **Follow competitors online:** Monitor their social media, websites, and announcements for insights into their strategies.
- **Use analytics tools:** Platforms like Google Trends and market research tools can help you identify emerging patterns.
- **Stay tuned to customer feedback:** Pay attention to reviews and customer comments to understand changing preferences.

2. Attend Networking Events and Trade Shows

Why they matter:

- **Learn from experts:** Gain knowledge from industry leaders, panel discussions, and keynote presentations.
- **Discover new tools and techniques:** Trade shows often showcase the latest technologies and trends.
- **Build relationships:** Networking with peers and potential collaborators can lead to partnerships or valuable advice.

3. Adapt Products or Services to Meet Evolving Customer Needs

- **Collect regular feedback:** Use surveys, reviews, and

direct communication to understand what your customers want.

- **Experiment with new ideas:** Test updates to your products or services through limited launches or pilot programs.
- **Stay flexible:** Be willing to pivot or enhance your offerings based on data and emerging trends.

Embrace Continuous Learning

1. Invest in Your Professional Development

Ways to invest in yourself:

- **Take online courses or workshops:** Platforms like Coursera, Udemy, and LinkedIn Learning offer affordable options for building new skills.
- **Attend industry conferences:** Stay updated on trends while networking with other professionals.
- **Read a wide selection of materials:** Books, case studies, and blogs written by successful entrepreneurs can provide invaluable insights.

2. Learn from Failures and Use Them as Growth Opportunities

- **Reflect honestly:** Identify what went wrong and why.
- **Extract lessons:** Look for insights that can help you improve your strategies.
- **Adjust and move forward:** Use what you've learned to refine your approach and try again.

3. Stay Curious and Experiment with New Strategies

- **Ask questions:** Always be looking for ways to improve or try something new.
- **Test different strategies:** Experiment with marketing approaches, products, or operational methods.
- **Encourage feedback:** Listening to employees and customers can spark creative solutions.

Avoid Burnout & Sustain Your Entrepreneurial Energy

1. Prioritize Self-Care and Work-Life Balance

- **Set boundaries:** Establish clear work hours and stick to them.
- **Take breaks:** Short daily breaks and occasional days off help you recharge.
- **Focus on wellness:** Regular exercise, a healthy diet, and adequate sleep improve both mental and physical health.

2. Delegate Tasks to Lighten Your Workload

Tips for effective delegation:

- **Identify tasks to offload:** Pinpoint repetitive or time-consuming activities that others can manage.
- **Leverage freelancers or assistants:** Platforms like Upwork or Fiverr make it easy to find affordable help.
- **Empower your team:** Trusting others to take ownership of tasks fosters collaboration and efficiency.

3. Celebrate Milestones to Stay Motivated

- **Set achievable goals:** Break larger objectives into smaller, trackable steps.
- **Recognize successes:** Have pizza or other food delivered to your workplace; go out to a fancy restaurant; provide gifts to staff etc.
- **Reflect on growth:** Take time to appreciate how far you've come, even during challenging times.

Building a Sustainable Business Model

Focus on Long-Term Customer Relationships

1. Foster Trust Through Transparency and Consistency

How to build trust:

- **Be transparent:** Clearly communicate policies, pricing, and any changes that affect customers.
- **Follow through:** Ensure that you deliver what you promise, every time.
- **Own mistakes:** If something goes wrong, address it honestly and take swift action to resolve it.

2. Reward Loyal Customers with Exclusive Benefits

- **Offer exclusive deals:** Provide discounts, early access to new products, or members-only perks.
- **Create a loyalty program:** Implement a points-based system or tiered rewards to incentivize continued engagement.
- **Recognize milestones:** Celebrate anniversaries or frequent purchases with personalized offers or thank-you messages.

3. Use Feedback to Continually Improve Offerings

How to leverage feedback:

- **Ask for input:** Use surveys, reviews, or direct conversations to gather insights.
- **Analyze feedback:** Look for patterns or recurring themes

to identify areas for improvement.
- **Act on suggestions:** Show customers that their opinions matter by implementing changes based on their feedback.

Reinforce Your Brand Identity

1. Stay Consistent in Messaging Across Platforms

- **Use a cohesive tone and style:** Ensure that your language, visuals, and design elements align across your website, social media, and marketing materials.
- **Stick to your core values:** Reflect the same principles in every customer interaction.
- **Develop a style guide:** Create a document that outlines your brand colors, fonts, and voice to keep messaging uniform.

2. Build a Reputation for Reliability and Quality

Steps to enhance reliability and quality:

- **Deliver consistently:** Meet or exceed customer expectations every time.
- **Respond promptly:** Address inquiries, complaints, and feedback with urgency and care.
- **Focus on excellence:** Regularly evaluate and refine your products or services to maintain high standards.

3. Strengthen Your Brand Story to Connect Emotionally with Customers

How to craft and share your story:

- **Highlight your "why":** Share the purpose behind your business—what drives you and how you're making a difference.
- **Use storytelling in marketing:** Share customer success stories, challenges you've overcome, or behind-the-scenes moments.
- **Align with customer values:** Show how your brand resonates with the aspirations or beliefs of your audience.

Plan For The Future

1. Set Five-Year Growth Goals and Milestones

Steps to create long-term goals:

- **Define specific objectives:** Break your vision into measurable milestones, such as revenue targets, customer growth, or product expansions.
- **Plan backward:** Determine the steps needed to reach each milestone and assign realistic timelines.
- **Review and adjust:** Regularly evaluate progress and adapt goals as needed to stay on track.

2. Explore Opportunities for Scaling Internationally or Digitally

Ideas for scaling:

- **International markets:** Research demand in new regions, adjust offerings to fit cultural preferences, and use global e-commerce platforms for accessibility.

- **Digital opportunities:** Develop online courses, subscription services, or digital products to reach broader audiences with minimal overhead.
- **Partnerships:** Collaborate with local or international partners to ease the transition into new markets.

3. Create a Succession Plan for Sustained Success

How to create a succession plan:

- **Identify potential successors:** Look for team members or external candidates who align with your vision and values.
- **Document processes:** Ensure workflows, policies, and key responsibilities are clearly outlined and accessible.
- **Train future leaders:** Provide mentorship and opportunities for growth to prepare the next generation of leadership.

Remember, the future starts with the actions you take today. Build a vision that inspires growth and a foundation that supports it.

Conclusion

Your Entrepreneurial Journey Awaits

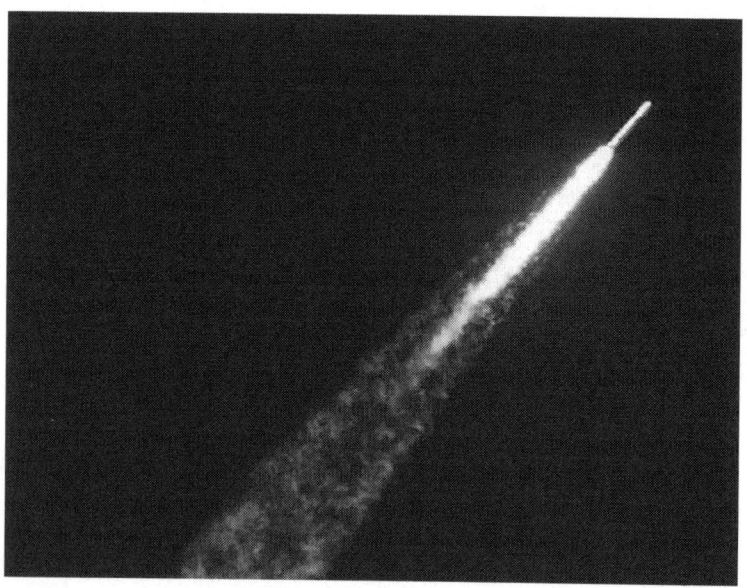

Launching and running a business on a tight budget requires creativity, discipline, and a commitment to continuous learning. But more than that, it requires belief in your vision and the courage to take the first step.

Remember, success doesn't come from having unlimited resources—it comes from making the most of the resources you have. By funding wisely, leveraging free and low-cost tools, and running lean operations, you'll not only build a business—you'll build a business that can thrive in times of adversity *and* prosperity.

So, what's next? It's time to put your plans into action. Follow the steps from this book, adapt them to your unique vision, and start creating the business you've always dreamed of. Launch boldly, dream big, and remember: you truly have no limits!

If this book has resonated with you, inspired you, or provided value in any way, I have a small request: please consider leaving a review on Amazon. Your feedback not only helps me as an author, but also helps other readers discover the book so they can follow along on how to launch & grow a business with limited resources.

Thank you for reading until the end. I wish you the very best!

Megan

Made in the USA
Columbia, SC
26 January 2025

52696450R00067